THE POETIC ZEAL

THE POETIC ZEAL

Caleiph Ken'yon Brewer

To order additional copies of this book, contact:
Xlibris Corporation
1-888-795-4274
www.Xlibris.com
Orders@Xlibris.com
36401

When you were a baby I'd grip your tiny hands with my fingers.
You'd always hold a firm clutch and would never
let go.
Audrey Keith Brown

Unlikely as it is to be a big fish in a small pond,
I continue to wonder. Hence the lesson of fingers,
I can swim in any direction of the wind.
Always love,
Your son

CONTENTS

PERSONAL REFLECTION

HAIKU

SOCIETAL

THE ARC OF PATRIOTISM

LOVE AND ARTS

Personal Reflection

"*The Quest*" painting by Michael Jaszczak,
Copyright 1986.

Quest

Life is a Journey,
There are many paths, only one door.
As I search for truth,
I'm confronted with beasts' confusion and horror.
Bombarded with shackles on my mind,
I find myself trapped in a terrible bind.
My visions vanished making me blind.
I yearn for escape into the light,
I just want to see what is right.
And So I Seek.

As I passionately search for affection;
I'm stormed by fear, deceit and rejection.
Leaving me a heart consumed with neglection.
It is the spirit of hope that soothes my unrest.
Like a dove; only love.
And So I seek.

Life is unpredictable.
Seasons change until the ending.
I've been shivering since the beginning!
The way of honor is what I desire.
I'll keep faith until the final hour.
I hear a voice, It whispers softly:
What you seek you'll find in thee.
So here I stand forever knowing,
The quest I seek starts with me.
And So I Seek.

Amour Propre

Like treasures on rowan trees,
Blossoming seeds appease.
Like liquids in motion of a Matrix scene,
An eye of foundation twines the structure of its streams.
Like indignity sabotages magnificence,
Roots nourish weeds that corrupt the psyche of the innocent.
As seeds grow in the wild they regard idle luxuries as prospect.
The inability to teach artificial norms from applicable wisdoms,
Deprives crops from its most instinctive tool known as self respect.

Beneath Billboards

In the arrays of animated text
pendulously upon a perch.
I esteem to espy
longer ends of a bird's broken bone.

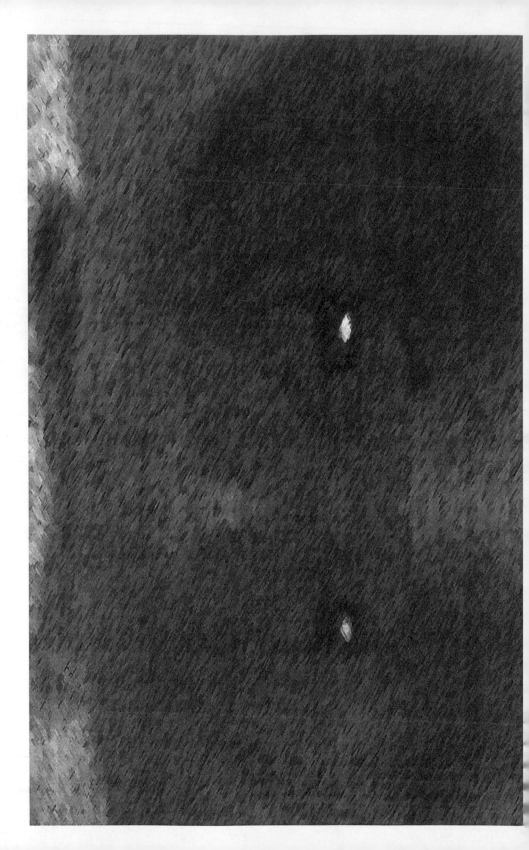

A pain in my eye

As minutes drop, I stand glazed to a mirror.
There I see a man, falling in the dark.
Like a rock in rivers, he looks so alone.
No family or friends, no love to his own.
With his hand over mouth
And a shortness of breath,
There's nothing much to say.
Deep thoughts of would could've been,
Tears never go away.
Massive the reflections of a scarred past.
Alive are guilts for how long they last.
Mercy upon him for he tried and tried.
The rein for relief, there is a pain in his eye!
He needs a shirt,
One to comfort away the cold.
In his soul I sense shivers, crumbling to fold.
The beacon of his youth, so long since old.
I want to help him, but it hurts.
It hurts to see his bruise.
Here's my hand! Here's my hand!
Take it if you choose.
They say a mirror changes.
It just isn't fair. Why am I still here?
And he's standing in there!
All I ever want is to escape the sorrow.
The Bacardi's in the cabinet,
Can it wait till tomorrow?

Still as I look into my eyes,
Only I can see.
Something so strong and beautiful,
The diamonds in me.
Still as I look into my eyes,
Only I can see!
Something so strong and beautiful,
The diamonds in me.

Twilight

Beaming in quantum's of mist,
      The spell of a dry verdant,
Entice a zigzagged urge.
      In clouds of a grown exhaust,
Paces of an enwrapped trance dazzle,
      As rubious eyes vent fission, a lull, a psyche,
      He mumbles:
Do you love me Mary Jane . . . Mary Jane!
      With blazed spirits of laughter,
For the thrill of the dome,
      Another hit followed thereafter.
Soon enough the break of dawn emerges
      And anneals his mind.
No longer suspended by troubles of day,
      Moments of a bittersweet arise.
Bells of reality annoy,
      While the eventual rule of night atones.
The dank grazed grass of sunset,
      Preludes a zone.

SF: The Café on Market Street

The kite erection of Friday night.
Like bees poised in hives,
In my bucket I buzz; prowling for a good time.
Sheering stiff out of place, I find myself in the Castro.
In cock prone boredom I park abut a fleece meter.
Discreetly like mice walking on eggs,
I leap across a herd of rainbows.

Fidgeting to the cliché of cliques;
The endowment of a beauty queen's crown,
The enchanting nudge of swingers passing by,
The fluidity of effeminate mouths,
And bums permeating an alley with Black
and Milds.
Adjoined en masses are clubbers
With the endearment of being swallowed,
A feeling Sima Qian could only fathom.

As I stumble through a crowd of blue.
I trip in an atrium stagnant to a roof.
Slanting upon menthol walls with a hand of whisk,
A bottle top's beam licks every drop of risk.
Beating and swirling like cows' are milked.
I toast with a bust to the floor.

Hunger

I'm Hungry,
And I want to eat.
I can see myself sitting in that hard-boiled chair,
Nibbling allspice and icings of a cinnamon crust.
I want to eat with the aqua green spoons,
Reflecting spiral fans; the same spoons my mom said:
Son, they aren't silver.

I'm Hungry,
And I want to eat.
I can foretaste that ravenous growl
Toughing and thawing through me
Like spasms of lemon steak sizzling on a grill.
Imaginably uneasy, I'm queasy enough to say
I'm in a fey and in need of an exorcism.

I'm Hungry,
And I want to eat.
As corrosions of internal lavas erupt,
In perspired patience, I tighten.
Finally, when I see that cherry oak roll
Replete with foggy mochas and caramel apple nuts,
Guess what? I will feast and tear it all up.

Tenors of spring

Outside a grape curtain,
And the tame combing of a garden's husk.
Is the branch of a benched patio,
Where I lay.
Drowsed in boughs of moist palms,
And spawning loaves of a lady bugged nest.
I riddle to the cadence of a herd's peck,
And the beige jig of a butterfly's punt.
Loose like pages of a clave,
I tingle to the foamed melt of an ice brew.
Inside me is the chant of a jungle,
Like the hoopla of a chimpanzee,
Jumping over panther piss.
So grotesque I've felt.
Laying in my backyard,
Raving for you to come outside.

Dysfunctional House

A family in tatters, a fawning interred.
Euphemisms speak with the utmost spite.
Arrows of hate, sad and absurd.
Grace for family appear so trite.

Euphemisms speak with the utmost spite,
Love is a pattern which fills the void.
Arrows of hate, sad and absurd,
Gone are joys hindered by fights.

Love is a pattern which fills the void,
Reconciliations make family again.
Gone are joys hindered by fights,
A family in tatters, a fawning interred.

Haiku

Aspiration

In taut, acumens
Eschew inner fecklessness
To reach perfection.

Perseverance

Able to be bent
Frankly made to be easy,
Brawl, pry, walk and rise.

Common Sense

Mundane reasoning
Exhibits matter to the
Gem of sound results.

Rule of thumb

Humbled reflexes
Softens the steep structured cloth
That keeps us stubborn.

Coin Flipper

In moderation
The laws of choice, not physics
Determines our deed.

Meditation

Plains and plateaus are
Meekly formed by flows of the
Invincible chi.

Antiques

A nova's nuance
Salient and silent had
Surged into vessels.

Traffic Watch

In circled ruckus
Morning strolls warp a village
With shrill sledging brims.

Ballroom Euphoria

In rite with fatigues
Capezio and Boateng
Relax and mambo.

(Inspired by the song *"Relax and Mambo"*
from Machito and his Afro-Cubans.)

Villa on deck

Season throttled yacht
Tropical fruit suited dolphs
Beguine and peach scotch.

A stern kneels constant
Troughs to dock is a fete
A fiddled Cugat.

A table scone melt
The flashing of Flinch cards dealt
Season throttled yacht.

Godsend Gospel

The fit robed choir
And its élan is where the
Heed become balanced.

For the all woman

If cook babe looked good
She would be no half-way house
Thus, misunderstood.

Drunkard Tantrum

Cemented zombies
Effused with unctuous poisons
Vented with venom.

House Chore

In the domicile
A pan and splintered leaf squeaks
While strands had all clapped.

Vanity

The smog of ego
Is so deft it can rid our
World of fervency.

Prunes and Prisms

Ridging athwart woods
With festoons and rice boutiques
Aghast she sprinkles.

Redolence

An influx of ferns
Surmounting the lambent sheen
Limn auras of myth.

Poetic Zeal

The craft voice of verve
In verse of revelation
I speak as poet.

Societal

Hierarchy

Upon the ladder
The austerity of prosperity
Is rigorously rich and vexing.
Its flexing candor despise and tantalize.
For the uninspired,
Its embedded pride is proportionally mental.
The fortunate however,
With a sloping thrust of peanuts
Deem marginal climbs until their stick breaks.

All Night Vigil

In a formidable dungeon,
I kneel to the burn of wavered wax.
Tinged by voids and unsparing taboo's,
Drenched in candescence,
      Thank God—it wasn't you.
A stampede clings to the mementos of daunt,
The paucity of noise, a community destroyed.
Common are these socials of solemn and distraught.
With intertwined fingers, I pray a safe heaven.
The dogmas of a barrel,
      He was only eleven.

God Bless Our Children

In the canoe of a winding solace,
Our pearls of promise embark new arrivals.
As they paddle the realms of playground,
Let not our rashes of hoary hands harm their gaiety.
For our pearls of promise are ribbons across the sky,
And the lamp to a dieing rain.

Letter to a dead President

Dear: President Thomas Jefferson.
Amid debacles of slavery
And its strain to the fragile south.
You suggest me as dull, tasteless.
Further censuring my existence
Short of reflection and in contrast sensational.
The sustained entourage of colonial hate
Enough to give Hitler hiccups
Is startling urban Black America.
Our worth in your theory
Is synonymous to a clubbing night stick
Reminding us of our place in the world.
In precedence of two-hundred years,
Nothings changed.
If we're not under a court and net
With a million dollar $mile,
$aying: Just Do It.
If we are not railing in the form of rap.
If we are not comically integrated
With the idée fixe of propaganda.
The assumption with regard to pigmentation
Is that we succumb to the stature of victimization.
Deprived forty achors and a mule
With no buns in my oven.
I ask even with your criticism of Phillis Wheatley,
How can I reprimand the societal anguish
of America?
Mr. President! Mr. President!

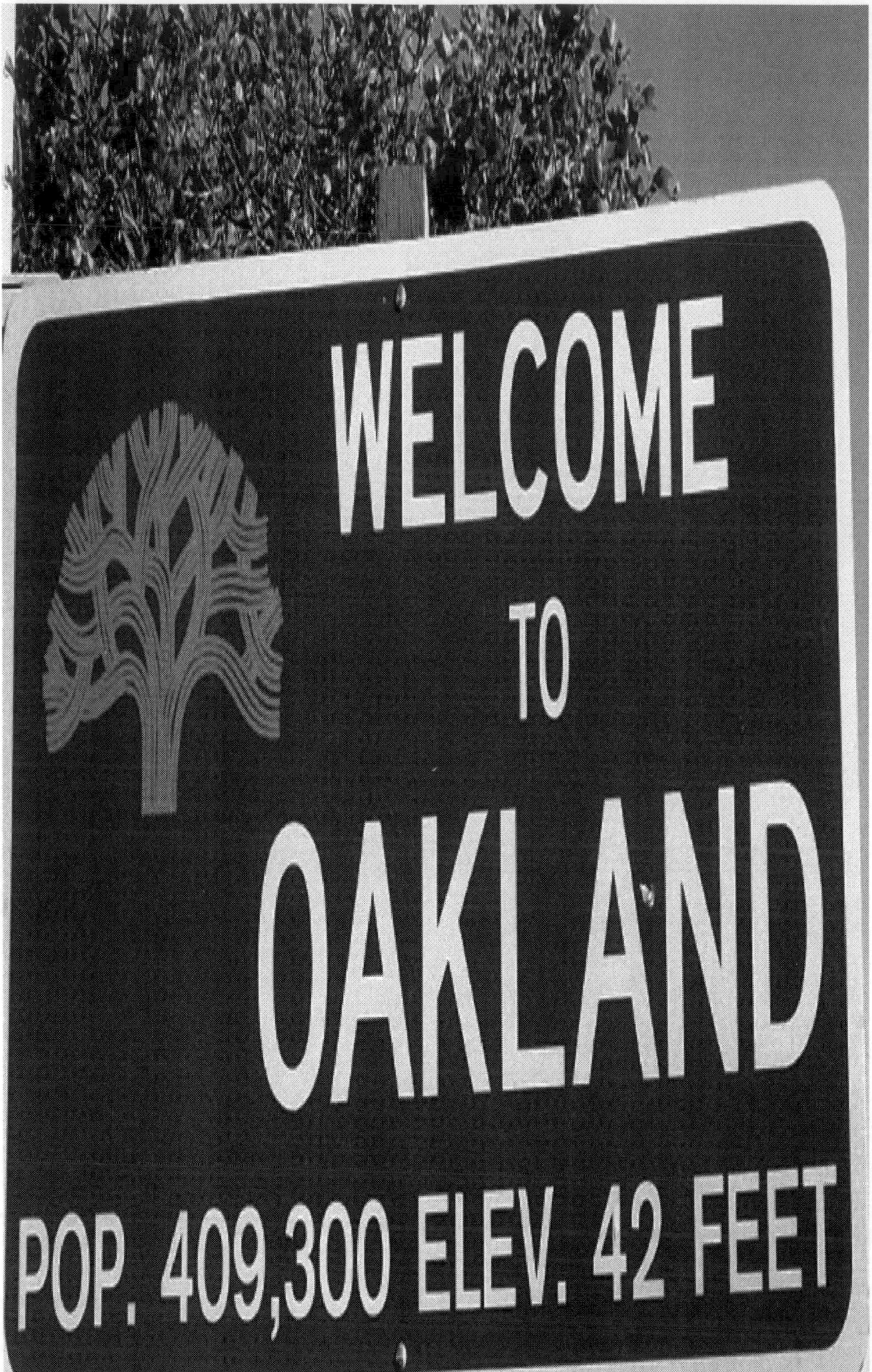
WELCOME
TO
OAKLAND
POP. 409,300 ELEV. 42 FEET

Lower Bottom

Life's phenomenon.
Sweet like the strike of a lustrous wand.
However I do remember times on the block.
West Oakland, in the cuts of Linden Street.
Pop! Pop! Pop! Ooh sporadic guns shots,
And metallic sounds of a magazine drop.
Sirens of cops and medics attempt to save an existence.
Knock-knock; Open up . . . it's the police!
        -No one cares to witness.
Here is something you can't understand.
They emptied the clip on that man!
Let me see my baby! Let me see him!
A mother cries in vain. Seeing ricochets on the ground awe,
I hate living in the ghetto; I can't stand this ghetto!
Yeah, I know. Me too maa.
Number ninety-eight they advertise,
        -Just another unsolved homicide.

        What's the meaning?
        What's the meaning of life?
Remembering and remembering times on the block.
West Oakland, in the cuts of Center Street.
Huey P. Newton shot and left for dead.
Once news got out, police and camera crews come about.
People from all over pay vigil for repose,
But who did it? Who did this?
        -Nobody knows.
Standing a mannequin in recluse,
Indentations of accusations unnerve,
While a woman in front of children hoses brains to the curb.

What's the meaning?
What's the meaning of life?
Sweet like the strike of a lustrous wand.
For you I'll share a secret, in my part of town
Black men are endangered,
Like species displayed in museums.
Did you see them? Why didn't we need them?
Could you survive if you were to be them?
Logicality of technicality is so sublime.
Miseries of societal constructs are just,
One beat shy to a flat line.
(Whistle.)
There goes my city of the nickel and dime.

Negotiated Education

Teach me some-some,
A missing syllable to a syllabus called thing.
Innuendos of education are so extreme.
Poor young minds experience racial isolation in classrooms it seems.
The conspiracy is curriculum, the convictions are merit schemes.

Military, prisons, death and drugs;
Discombobulating paths putting us on edge.
Why aren't more of us in college instead?
The rich discern that our youth can't learn.
Isn't that ironic? Ebonics!
The problems are economic.

The qualities of academics swirl,
Round and round like the mime of squirrels looking for a nut.
Get it, get it! Tackle, hut, hut! Winning teams mean green,
No worries of a seasoned pay cut.

Underrepresented,
It's wrong, so wrong.
Regurgitated texts are like a game of ping pong.
I hate how diaries of politics prolong.
Pricey overrated tuitions are rising, higher and higher.
A teacher's worst error—leading students into dire.

I'm not asking for handouts,
I'll coast for all heights.
I am asking for opportunity
Entitled to most Whites.
Like sputniks in space recon the globe,
Knowledge is key to the doors we probe.
So for the students deserve, stack away the reserves.
Teach me something about life,
I haven't already herd.

Cultural Normality

Five-hundred dollar FUBU attire, eight-teen carrot gold figaros.
Five-minute whores hiding in bushes looking for candy.
Deadbeat dads living up under mama, and single parent moms,
High of welfare drama. To be Black you must be this.

Trend of such assertions rumble me, like the rocking of a ritcher
scale.
That's when I start dropping poetry, like munitions of artillery
To blow the sickening prejudice right off of you.

Stymied by suppositions and the status qou of conditions
On what being Black is; I am often painted in colors of being washed,
Confused, insensible and lost in an identity crisis.
Treatment of indifference in my name sends me grief
Since I am no Ronald, No Eric, No Thomas,
But Caleiph.

And yes if you ask,
If you are Black, you do go back.
Back to the far end statistic line
When the twisted urban thug in you help decide
A college education isn't cool to you.

You do go back.
Back to the master who made you watch
As brothers were disciplined under whip and ropes.
The same master whose agenda was to call you nigger.
Yet you have the audacity to spit in my face
With that watered down term called nigga
And presume I take such greet as compliment.
When in fact the decadent remark is clearly a stigma
Depicted in our generation we understand as (X)enophobic.

The forlorn effigy of Black characterization
Framed by insensitive politics and invested hype
Has minimized an entire era of innovation.
Such as the creations and inspirations
Of Hughes, Ellison, McKay and Wright.
Pioneers who paved the right for me to write.
So don't lecture me on whom or what I should be.
I am who I am and moving toward degree.
My cultural normality.

Hard Economics

Minimum
stiff, broke
bitching, grinding, struggling
shrink, shrug, crop, choke
distressing, transgressing, repressing
heartless, difficult
Wage.

Pickets across a Nation

Within the powdered scores of occupation
And across passages of the four directions
Are the fenced halls of Montezuma.
Around sealed wharfs and the autumn of Ellis Island
Are eager footprints that trailed to enfranchise.
Under shades of reform and constraints
And through equanimities of decade long debates
We are confronted with concertinas of real politic.
Through the laurel and datum's of constitution
Our paralleled reach for the human dream
Is conventionally divided,
As is the ideal in being American.

On Elian Gonzalez

North America and Cuba.
Between our seas' sprinkling voice,
Lays this compendium:
A whirling fantasy; it's all they've known.
Crossing watery notions of a nation divide.
Requiems for how their travel ended.
Elian left alone, his mom rescinded.

The distant families like a harrier's hurdle,
Fleet to a visions' advent.
Surveillances survey the S.W.A.T's moxie,
Demising a clause's intent.

Asylum for the young island eyes,
That is all the family wanted.
Surviving magnet of origin,
Comforts Elian and the publics.

In memoria of the cold our jurisdictions relent.
For the eyes of his son and court appeals.
He applauds the time half-spent.
For U.S a tearful cloth waves.
What, really; did it meant?

Field of view

Picture if only you will,
A calm potion in a vase.
The grant of an innate wish,
Bounding to a better place.
Roguish in our appearance,
Giveth a mode of rebirth.
Behold if only you will,
A cosmic intemperance.
Loyalty of fellow man,
No more iron peddled thick.
Just imagine if you can.

Kindred Spirit

Shall I only survive through ink,
Our maternals' rising waves will recede,
Along with the feuds she cries to.

Shall I only survive through ink,
A truce will exist among brothers in the East.
The deliriums of famine and droughts will cease.

Shall I only survive through ink,
Judge me not on my adage,
But by the heart captioning through me.

For I am no deity and like all things,
Parting the continuums of a drum;
The semblance, I hold will one day molder.

If it's not asking too much,
This vision of world peace will prevail.
Shall I only survive through ink.

The Arc of Patriotism

Infamous Bearing

Profligacy raised the right hand,
Folded wrongly and wrongly pummeled.
Their beleaguered barricades;
Unchaste protocols, frenzies and brute
Reflect immodesty of legitimate conduct.
Antecedently civility suffered the senseless carnage.
In zephyr of righteousness through casts of perilous woes,
I render to the songless nightingale.

Omen

Inaugurated greed and miscalculated sanity.
Squint declarations of caution.
Itches of panic and equivocations of fact.
Haste judgments and altitudes of fear.
Preemptive measures with extreme outcomes.
Inbound spheres of an explosive sun.

Deployment

The night of lasting impressions.
Family and friends greet prayers and goodbyes.
Hugs and kisses engross fears, some of us will die.

Why lingers the reasoning of one's troubled mind?
Admonitions of a noble soul said: Your time is your time.
Head over heels for you were told: This is just a tour.
Concealed hysteria helps bear the fact.
We're going off to war.

In the early morning formation,
I stand stern to a nation's calling.
The stories and sacrifices before me,
Are grave and appalling.

For the work of God I mustn't fear.
Rodger First Sergeant, I'm here!
For those in the rear, I'll see you in a year.

On the bus I ponder,
Killing enemies in the prone.
One shot, one kill! We're in this together,
We'll find our way home.

Habbinayah

Here in light of methodic movement,
we have our history.

As we cross the ragged Kuwaiti borders,
defunct sweat and hot air are the fruits of our labor.

Bottleneck roads drive suspicion,
as shady gestures greet.

Bound to the integrity of motto,
we remain athirst to our mission's aim.

In perpetual wonder,
we're acquainted to resounding idioms
as we gaze the Milky Way.

Nearing the midst of travel,
we roar as hilos fly overhead.

As a mere surprise, we witness destruction,
caused by the art of one's lore.

Yet amid threats of danger,
animals grant mute amusements.

At last we arrive on camp,
there the Colonel says:

Hooaah! Centurions,
harvest this camp, and breathe.
Make no mistake, we'll be here until we leave.

Inferno

Grace under fire, a dispositional stage.
As temperatures rise,
Heat draws the weary into a fierce rage.
Ode to the crime wave,
Mobsters, murderers . . . all of the depraved.
Boom! Sounds the gage;
Another cradle to the grave.
The Ogre scorns raucously as he devoirs a
jaded pact.
Demonic voices echo during the craft of
haunt's design.
Premonitions of doom in the eyes of prey
woefully react.
Possessions, ruins and illusions mark the souls once left behind.
Quivered veins, jagged chains and burning
flesh pervade.
Aromas of death and furnace, court a
hellish masquerade.
Blood shot tears drop as danger excites the screams.
A new world order?
Odds are beyond the means.
Pursuits of peace and consolation,
Only memories of a dream.

Never Forget
These Extraordinary Warriors.

Paying Homage

First Lieutenant TODD J. BRYANT
Sergeant UDAY SINGH
Specialist ROGER G. LING
Second Lieutenant JEFFREY C. GRAHAM

Our greatest sacrifices.
From all walks of life.
They were husbands, sons, fathers
They are brothers.
Brothers who did not lose their lives
They gave their lives.
They were defenders of a nation, family and free.
Oh, say can you see,
A democracy indeed.
Liberty and justice
The hands that feed.
With these men we marched
Soldiers to shoulder.
And in the voice of O.N.E
We sung over and over.
In voices we no longer hear,
We will never forget the dignity of their duty.
And in their sake,
We realize their way of courage and sacrifice
Can Only Be Read As Separable.
Our greatest sacrifices.
Strong to lead, brave to bleed.
Always, Cobras.
The ones to carry through.

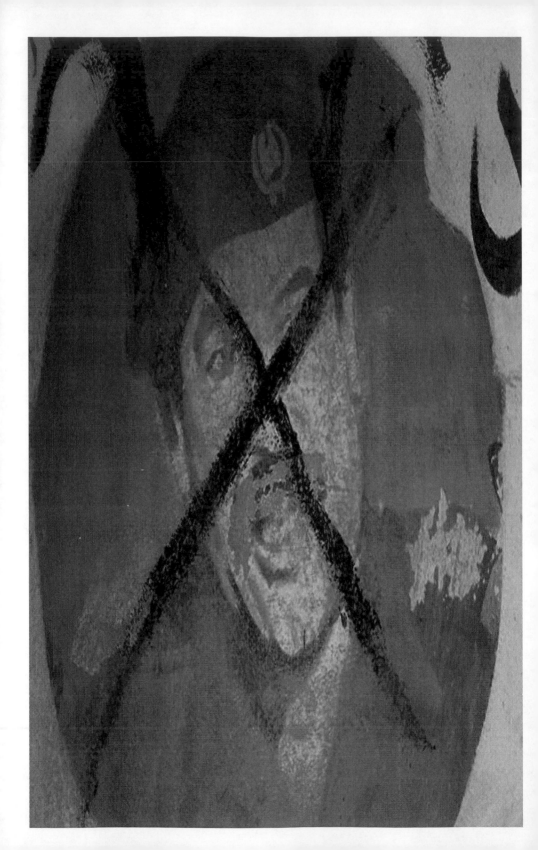

Non Compos Mentis

The Martyr of Abu sought vengeance.
Blasphemous in faith,
An insurgence distortion of Hajj
Tethered blind folds and thunder on beheaded men.
Must such imbeciles hide
Like girdle shoveled near Euphrates,
The feline persistence for justifiable
resolve is steadfast.
Imminently,
The wicked upshot of barbarism
Ineludibly should surface as unviable in cause;
Unaccomplished in effect.

Survivor's Guilt

In languish moments
Jarringly facing the sink
Numb, battered, abashed
Unfit to shed any grief
Taps so dense quaver and mourn.

Airborne B-767 Convoy

Hover the gates and wait!
A paved eternity naively chased.
Trundling from a shielded row,
Bridging gaps of a year ago.
On the plane the feeling dramatic,
To be alive the triumph ecstatic.
As silent ceruleans struck chins,
Labored cargos locked to skin.
From lands to skies, sighs and sighs.
No more darts and race car bombs,
An engine's ambiance assures calm.
Landing in tan, there's no more sand.
Just roads and roads, our peace at hand.
Parting the fallen, worry and wrath,
At ease, twenty seconds!
Reveille at last.

Love and Arts

Mambo Sentimental

Flouncing joyously
Urbane from collar to heel
Lewd and vivacious
Airs of bugle ivory
Liberate furor and hope.

Latin Jazz Passion

Listening.
As I sway to the breeze of tongue,
Congas sing the hymn of culture.
While the bass electrifies moods,
The piano captivates a majestic encore.
Blended with range,
Lively timbales are spatulas of sound.
As suave saxophones heightens melodramatic twists;
Maracas invigorate cunningly,
Like a snake's rattle and hiss.
As raised violins breathe a subtle whine,
Mingling vibes drift like balms of pine.
While whistling to songs and dynamic melodies,
Ever so delicately, I dance as music bleeds.

Promethean

In sketch of a thinking masterpiece,
there lies an affinity to a metaphor.
Adaptively, the aesthetics of canvassing,
press and crease the posh of a new portrait.

Podium and Poet

Restful and resolute as a soothsayer's fable,
Technician of meter, rhyme and sound,
The affects of words, voice and table.

Sharing in the world of Cain and Able,
Usefulness of pace, tone and style,
Restful and resolute as a soothsayer's fable.

Pin, paper and words are banal,
Truth in diction seems so mien,
The affects of words, voice and table.

Shriving audiences like babies in a cradle,
Tooling nature like moldings of clay,
The affects of words, voice and table.

Focused thoughts, steady, stable,
Procuring ethos with vision and precision,
Restful and resolute as a soothsayer's fable.

Aesthetics, practice, time, origination.
In admiration of imagination,
Hubs so vast thrive in April.
The affects of words, voice and table.

On Nights Like This

On nights like this
A moon yokes in the abyss.
Serene to the delicious amber night,
Punctuated stars are a romantic ecstasy.
Like a lullaby
I feel a flame next to me.
Obsessing I think of you
My warming bliss.

Under the bed of restless hands,
I can no longer withstand.
Lonesome and loveless
I yield a script for you;
On nights like this.

I reminisce those days,
On how we kick it in our ways.
Foreshadowed without you
I am an eclipse in view.
A gift without gist
On nights like this.

In these words, Italian

Oh sweet lady, young fetish of mine.
Don't ask why for I don't know how.
The college life is what started it all.
We met in need, just strangers in the crowd.
In the august night I approached you; Ciao!
Shined like a medallion; your smile brightens doubts.
First base complete;
         So then I said:
         l'amore, il mio amore è venuto a me.
         This in Italian . . . come go with me.
         Voglio essere con lei.

Like the watch of an owl; meticulously and curiously.
I stared into the howling of your silhouette dress.
With a gentle slow motioned touch,
I caress your cheeks and kissed you on the hand.
Your curved tender hips ingenuously laced with mine.
To the dance floor we go,
The music was fast, then it got slow
Let's go to my room. Ok, hint!
Your fragrant fixings stimulate senses,
The sparks of your eyes invite intimacy.
Fascinated by sexual anatomies I clasp your breasts.
With adrenalines rushing the room we undress.
In finesse your hands slithered onto my chest.
Yes! Yes . . . And we proceed to progress.
         So Then I said:
         l'amore, il mio amore è venuto a me.
         This in Italian . . . come go with me!
         Voglio essere con lei.

Fondling, I knead you from neck to waste.
Upon the moments climax,
I lave your barren glands.
You justify comfort in soft indistinct moans,
As I manipulate horizons.
Intersecting satisfactions communicate
The essence of an aphrodisiac—love.

So Then I said:
l'amore, il mio amore è venuto a me.
This in Italian . . . come go with me!
Voglio essere con lei.

You are the one I want.
Come go with me, come go with me.
Let's spend our lives in mere harmony.

Los Sentimientos Están Allí
(The feelings are there)

Slipping in the epitome for how things used to be.
I was all for you, you were once for me.
Alongside thrones of an endless repulse,
La perfidia en las dias y bien por las noches.
        Los sentimientos están allí,
The feelings are still there.

Unsettled by your eviction
I feverishly hang aloud.
Para ti y siempre, tu es el mundo a mí.
Even though my throbbing wings gasp
Over holes you carved in me.
        Los sentimientos están allí,
The feelings are still there.

With soul bursts of born dead pain
In cascades I drown,
Reaching for marveled time.
        Los sentimientos están allí,
Again, the feelings are still there.

I try to move on,
But something comes to mind . . .

Confide with this

I once touched your lips,
Kissed in days past.
Your vinegar lisped pose,
Proved a fond didn't last.
I touched your heart with mine,
Cognition of verity held inside.
Sinless utters of fidelity,
The dolls for my bride.
You said, you herd it all before.
There you go embracing the door.
Fact of matter, you love no more.
Our manifest to trust.
Give it time. You'll see.
Believe in the kiss you give.
Then come and touch me.

Equipoise Mint

The adore of equipoise mint
Climbs harmoniously in my shed.
With charcoaled beads and threading,
Its' sleeves and grazing shadows
Are the warmth of Highland's Pass.
Its voice celestial like wind upon rings.
Its pheromones soft and sweet
Like the dawn coconuts sing.
With an extravagant smile of hue and divines.
Unable to toe the line.
I lounge many wonders of fate.
Can it be? Can it be not?
Will the buds in my lungs expand and unknot?
Loves me, loves me not.
Loves me, loves me not.
Sudden echoes as dandelions flock.
Out of chance I lance to
The goodness I met today.
Equipoise Mint! Equipoise Mint!
Oh no, She went away.

Between Sheets

Human
kinky, randy
sniffing, licking, twitching
leak, stink, slap, rub
sucking, roughing, cussing
numbness, maximus
Nature.

Acknowledgements

Works Published:

- Timepieces Volume IV: Edited by JMW Publishing Company, summer 2006
Poem: "*On Nights Like This*"
- Best Poems and Poets of 2005: Edited by Howard Ely, spring 2006
Poem: "*Confide With This*"
- Treasury of American Poetry III: Edited by Teresa Starks, spring 2006
Poem: "*In these words, Italian*"
- Treasury of American Poetry II: Edited by Teresa Starks, fall 2005
Poem: "*Amour Propre*"
- Reflections: Edited by Maggie Whitford, fall 2005.
Poem: "*Inferno*"
- Poetry Vibes: Edited by Nancy M Johnston, spring 2005.
Poem: "*Deployment*"
- Written In dedication to task force 1st Battalion, 34th Armor, U.S ARMY.
- A Surrender To The Moon: Edited by Howard Ely, spring 2005.
Poem: "*Latin Jazz Passion*"
- Written in dedication to the SJSU Latin Jazz Ensemble.
- VoicesNet Journal: (www.voicesnet.org) winter, 2005.
Poem: "*HABBINAYAH*"
- Written In dedication to task force 1st Battalion, 34th Armor, U.S ARMY.
- The Spartan Daily: Opinion Section, May 5th 2004.
Poem: "*Quest*"
- Written in dedication to "*The Quest*" painting by Michael Jaszczak,
- Sigma Nu Fraternity, Delta Alpha chapter.

Praise God for the blessings of purpose and gift. To my mother Audrey Brown and father Ronald Brown. To my sisters Jessica Brown and Stacey Brown. Dr. Wade Nobles and aunt Vera L. Nobles. Thanks to "Muah" Jessie Wilson, may you forever rest in peace. Ruben Christovale my "soul brother" since Berkeley High. To Ms. Signe Mattson—the best English teacher I've ever had. Thanks to Sergeant. Robert Dedeaux, your ears and advice were an integral part of this project. To Charlie Company 1-34th Armor 1st Brigade 1st Infantry Division—Always Cobras; and a salute extends to all U.S. service members—Through your shield and sacrifice we are all free. To all brothers of Sigma Nu Fraternity—our precepts of LHT are a science transcending all boundaries; creating our rock of Brotherhood. Brother Darin Steven Gile thanks for extending the helping hand. To my music Professor Ray Castello for teaching me the repertoire of Cuban sound. To "The father of Latin Jazz," Mario Bauza—the elation felt in your music inspired me in more ways I can imagine. Finally I would like to thank all artists who thrive in venues of expression through words, symbols and imagination.

Biography

Caleiph Ken'yon Brewer was born on September 15 1977 in Berkeley California. His mother Audrey Brown and father Ronald Brown raised him along with his sister Jessica Brown in Oakland California. Surrounded by masses of crime, police brutality and others sores of society; Caleiph's vision centered on becoming a pioneer in and of his time.

Living impoverished brought about many changes for Caleiph—particularly with his education. Realizing the unjust plagues within the Oakland school system, Caleiph's mother filed an inter-district permit so that he could attend schools in Berkeley.

In 1990 he was granted to enroll at Willard Jr. High and graduated in 1992. In the same year, he enrolled at Berkeley High school and the roller coaster of his life was to begin.

Holding leadership in several capacities, Caleiph's contribution to Berkeley High and the community was remarkable. In 1994 he served as a staff writer for his school's publication (The Jacket). In 1995, Caleiph served as President of his founded Ethnomusicology Club. In 1996, he graduated Berkeley High commendably with scholastic recognition. His honors include the PG&E (Black Employees Association Scholarship), Morris and Juliet James Achievement Award, and a R.E.S.P.E.C.T oratical award.

In the fall of 1999, Caleiph attended San Jose State University and served as director of development for the Karate Club. The following semester he joined Sigma Nu Fraternity.

In 2003, he enlisted in the U.S Army for a term of three years. After completion of basic training, he was stationed in Fort Riley, Kansas and assigned to 1st Brigade 34th Armor. No longer then three months of his arrival to his active unit, he deployed to Iraq for a combat tour of one year. After returning stateside from combat operations, he was honorably discharged with Army commendation and achievement medals for his service and conduct.

Established in numerous anthologies and publications, Caleiph is continuing his education at San Jose State University majoring in criminal sociology.